Big Government: Myth or Might?

THE M. L. SEIDMAN MEMORIAL
TOWN HALL LECTURE SERIES

MEMPHIS STATE UNIVERSITY

The M. L. Seidman Memorial Town Hall Lecture Series was established by P. K. Seidman in memory of his late brother, M. L. Seidman, founder of the firm Seidman and Seidman, Certified Public Accountants.

Publication of this eleventh Series of Seidman Lectures was made possible by a gift from Mr. P. K. Seidman to the Memphis State University Press.

The M. L. Seidman Memorial Town Hall Lecture Series

1966–67 *Financial Policies in Transition*
edited by Dr. Thomas O. Depperschmidt

1967–68 *The USSR in Today's World*
edited by Dr. Festus Justin Viser

1968–69 *The News Media — A Service and a Force*
edited by Dr. Festus Justin Viser

1969–70 *Taxation — Dollars and Sense*
edited by Dr. Festus Justin Viser

1970–71 *The University in Transition*
edited by Dr. Festus Justin Viser

1971–72 *China's Open Wall*
edited by Dr. Festus Justin Viser

1972–73 *Crime and Justice*
edited by Dr. Festus Justin Viser

1973–74 *The Social Conscience of Business*
edited by Dr. Phineas J. Sparer

1974–75 *The World Today*
edited by Dr. Phineas J. Sparer

1975–76 *America: Heritage and Horizons*
edited by Dr. Phineas J. Sparer

Big Government: Myth or Might?

edited by Phineas J. Sparer

MEMPHIS STATE UNIVERSITY PRESS　　　1977

Robert . , Library

OCT 25 1978

Tallahassee, Florida

Copyright © 1978 Memphis State University Press
All Rights Reserved

Library of Congress Cataloging in Publication Data

Main entry under title:

Big government, myth or might?

(The M. L. Seidman memorial town hall lecture series; 1975-1976)
CONTENTS: Rostow, W. W. The public and private sectors in the fifth Kondratieff upswing. — Safire, W. Big government. — Seidman, L. W. Big government and the international economic scene.
1. United States — Economic policy — Addresses, essays, lectures.
2. International economic relations — Addresses, essays, lectures.
I. Sparer, Phineas J.   II. Rostow, Walt Whitman, 1916-
III. Safire, William L.   IV. Seidman, Lewis William.   V. Series.

HC103.B52   338.973   78-3729
ISBN 0-87870-041-2

Contents

Preface and Acknowledgements ix

Lecture One
"The Public and Private Sectors in the Fifth Kondratieff Upswing"
by Walt Whitman Rostow

1

Lecture Two
"Big Government"
by William Safire

21

Lecture Three
"Big Government and the International Economic Scene"
by L. William Seidman

35

Coordinating Committee

FESTUS J. VISER, DIRECTOR
    Professor of Economics
    Memphis State University

ROBERT T. GARNETT, ASSISTANT DIRECTOR
    Program Coordinator for
    Public Service and Continuing Education
    Memphis State University

FRANK R. AHLGREN
    Retired Editor
    Memphis Commercial Appeal

JERRY N. BOONE
    Vice President for Academic Affairs
    Memphis State University

FRED P. COOK
    Operations Manager
    WWEE Radio Station

MRS. CLARENCE H. FISHER
    Member Tennessee
    Higher Education Commission

KURT F. FLEXNER
    Chairman, Department of Economics
    Memphis State University

M. M. GORDON
    President
    Gordon Transports Inc.

ABE PLOUGH
    Chairman of the Board
    Plough, Inc.
    Chairman of the Board
    Schering Plough Corporation

P. K. SEIDMAN
    Partner
    Seidman and Seidman CPA

GAINES F. KEENER
    Partner
    Seidman and Seidman CPA

PHINEAS J. SPARER
    Emeritus Professor
    College of Medicine
    University of Tennessee Center for the
    Health Sciences

Big Government: Myth or Might?

Preface

For the 1975-1976 series, the eleventh in the M. L. Seidman Memorial Town Hall Lectures sponsored by Memphis State University, the Coordinating Committee chose the rather enigmatic theme, *Big Government: Myth or Might?* and three distinguished panelists were selected: Dr. Walt Whitman Rostow, author and advisor to President John F. Kennedy and President Lyndon B. Johnson; William Safire, author, former senior White House speechwriter and a Washington-based columnist of the *New York Times*; and Congressman Morris K. Udall, progressive spokesman and recent candidate for the Democratic presidential nomination. Congressman Udall had to withdraw as panelist because of a date conflict with a government mission. In his place, the Committee was fortunate to secure L. William Seidman, former consultant to the Republican Party in Washington and White House Economist.

Big government, as historic evidence indicates, has evolved from pre-industrial to comtemporary industrial America. This gradual development has proceeded pari passu with socio-economic growth and the maturation of modern capitalism. By the turn of the present century, federal government personnel and functions increased markedly due to extensive transformation evident in several areas of the American economy and in corporate political power. The federal government, already seriously and reasonably concerned with the control or regulation of economic life, also had to expand and increase its activities and employees to meet the new problems and projects that were forthcoming. But business people have been inclined to regard the government's requirements for control or regulation of economic pursuits as interposition in business affairs, as meddling with the compelling creed of freedom, the American way of life, with laissez-fairism, with Adam Smith's Invisible Hand of the market-place—a principle that relies on strictly defined "perfect competition."

There are people to whom big government is a euphemism for that part of the government that they don't like. There are others to whom a large part of big government is a bureaucracy with excessive authority or power in many functions of federal administration. Yet common sense tells many of us that big government can be made good government. After all, people and circumstances make big government, and make it meaningful.

Walt Whitman Rostow, the first panel speaker, born in New York city, 1916, has distinguished himself both in education and government service. Currently he is Professor of Economics and History, The University of Texas at Austin, where he teaches courses in Economic history and American diplomatic history. He was formerly Harmsworth Professor of American History at Oxford, 1945-1946; Pitt Professor at Cambridge, 1949-1950; and Professor of Economic History, Massachusetts Institute of Technology, 1950-1961.

After being a Rhodes Scholar from 1936 to 1938 at Balliol College, one of the oldest Oxford Colleges, he received the Ph.D. degree in 1940 from Yale University where he also received the AB degree in 1936. Shortly thereafter, he became an Instructor in Economics at Columbia University. Among his many prominent government positions, he has served as Assistant to the Executive Secretary of the Economic Commission for Europe (1947-1949); Staff member of the M.I.T. Center of International Studies (1951-1961); Counselor of our

Department of State and Chairman of its Policy Planning Council; United States representative and ambassador, The Inter-American Commission, Alliance for Progress (1964-1966). During World War II, he served as a major in the Office of Strategic Services.

In January 1961, he was appointed Special Assistant for National Security Affairs to President John F. Kennedy, and later the same position under President Lyndon B. Johnson. Rostow was the recipient of the Presidential Medal of Freedom (with distinction) in 1969 and his duties at the White House ended in January of that year. He was decorated Legion of Merit in 1945 and received the Order of British Empire in the same year.

Rostow has been a prolific and profound author of important books that project fresh light on various domestic and world problems. Among the books that have made him famous are:

The United States in the World Arena (1960), a readable and scholarly work dealing in recent history, considered to "have had more influence on United States' foreign policy than any work published in the past decade."

The Stages of Economic Growth —A Non-Communist Manifesto (1960), which records economic growth of certain societies on the basis of a dynamic theory of production, but his theory of production is in contrast to the Marxist Theory and the Communist Manifesto. Rostow also applies his hypothesis to possibilities for global peace.

Politics and the Stages of Growth (1970), in which Rostow pursues his analysis of economic growth but the focus is shifted to politics and the examination of the political intent and content of each of the stages experienced in developed and developing nations of today.

He edited *The Economics of Take-off into Sustained Growth* and is co-author of several works, including *The Dynamics of Soviet Society, The Prospects for Communist China*, and *An American Policy in Asia*. His recent books include *How It All Began: Origin of the Modern Economy*, and *The Diffusion of Power*.

Rostow's lecture is captioned: "The Public and Private Sectors in the Fifth Kondratieff Upswing". This historical and interesting overview of the role of the public and private sectors in our national life, is a tribute to our great society which started in President Washington's time from a quasi-partnershipi between the public and private sectors. Through the years, this partnership of public and private sectors proved to be effective, but every one of the many cooperative tasks "had its flaws and costs"; and there was always "legitimate reason for debate at the margin concerning the appropriateness of one or another form of public intervention in the economy." Rostow states that one of his prejudices or value judgments is a belief that a private, competitive free enterprise system is intrinsically better than a system of public enterprise. He considers it more consistent with human freedom; and public enterprises have a considerable capacity to survive even when using resources inefficiently, as many countries have demonstrated.

Nevertheless, Rostow specifies that the tasks of both our public and private sectors have radically changed in the past four years; and that the vitality of our society in the future depends on our understanding the changes and our consequently acting in new ways.

During his lecture, Rostow pointed out the relevance of trend periods, particularly the cycles associated with the Russian Economist, N. D. Kondratieff. According to Rostow, "the key lesson from history about Kondratieff upswings is exceedingly simple: to maintain an industrial society in the face of relatively expensive basic products, it is necessary to increase investment in ways which will expand the supply of those basic products or economize their use . . . the pattern of investment, the directions of investment must change." As Rostow sees it, the task ahead is a massive increase in investment in pertinent directions through the collaboration of the public and private sectors, with governments here and abroad intricately involved in policy towards energy, agriculture, raw materials, the environment, research and development. In all of that, the first duty of public policy is to set a framework for private enterprise to do a maximum job. Second, public policy could also help by offering special tax incentives and other forms of indirect public aid. Third, consideration should be given for increased incentives to expand private research and development, in the universities as well as in the business community. The government will have residual direct responsibilities in certain limited areas. Reading the details will be quite enlightening to the interested reader of Rostow's text.

To improve the quality of our society, to promote a sound economy, to overcome inflation and unemployment, his special message to friends in Washington is this: develop a public-private investment program, like the one in the text; put the economy on a path of sustained rapid growth and structural adjustment; develop new methods of public-private cooperation, along with a new spirit of doing this in the national interest; and in Rostow's words: "We may need an intellectual revolution as profound as the Keynesian Revolution itself."

In considering future perspectives and goals, now that the United States has come of age, Rostow concludes: "I have no doubt a fruitful new phase in the old public-private partnership is within our grasp," a conclusion presumably that his special message to Washington friends will bring salutary results.

William Safire, a native of New York City, is well-known as a conservative newspaper columnist and author. He attended Syracuse University and in 1949, at 20 years of age, began his career in journalism as a reporter for the *New York Herald Tribune*. In 1951 he became the Europe and Middle East correspondent for WNBC/WNBT. After his military service (1952-1954), he was the radio-television producer for NBC, New York City (1954-1955). As a public relations executive, he served as Vice President of TEX McCrary, Inc. (1955-1960); President of Safire Publication Relations, Inc. (1960-1968); and Special Assistant to President Richard Nixon as well as senior White House speechwriter for four years, during which time he was both trusted and wiretapped. In 1973, Safire joined the staff of *The New York Times* as a Washington-based columnist. His twice-weekly column, "Essay," is syndicated in more than 100 newspapers throughout the world and he has been hailed as a "fresh new voice" in American journalism.

William Safire's most recent non-fiction book (1975): *Before the Fall—An Outside View of the Pre-Watergate White House* is truly a republican's and conservative's portrayal that has been considered "unashamed to be sympathetic and unafraid to be critical." His other books include: *The Relations of Explosion* (1963); and *Plunging into Politics* (1964), which is co-authored.

The New Language of Politics (1968), a unique, handy and fascinating political dictionary established him as a discerning lexicographer. A thoroughly updated revised edition was published in 1972, *Full Disclosure—A Novel* (1977), is Safire's first venture into fiction; availing himself of intimate White House details only an insider knows, he ably portrays human beings caught in the web of contemporary political stresses and "outrageous fortune."

Safire, the second panelist, spoke briefly and informally from few notes, but not without thought-provoking ideas. He referred to the topic of Big Government as dear to his heart because he has been inveighing against it for years; and he directed attention to the tie clasp he was proudly wearing because it displayed the engraved name of former President Nixon. It was quite obvious that Safire perceives Nixon totally in sympathetic light, with high esteem for him both as a person and president. But as Safire indicates "in terms of big government, there's a bureaucratic mind-set that afflicts everyone. It's a bad thing. It's a necessary concomitant to big government." He has come to realize that he can always be certain about one thing, the steady growth of big government, which he characterizes as pernicious and sapping not only the American spirit but American business; and he gives some statistics of the steadily accelerating growth of big government which becomes streamlined with bureaucratism: "If we take that curve and project it at the current rate of growth, by the year 2000, 50% of the GNP will be paid in taxes, and 25% of the people in the labor force will be working for government. Now, that's the welfare state. That's a strangulated economy ... something that should alarm every American ..." There is no doubt that Safire believes in the slowing of the growth of Big Government and that this will redound to the people's benefit.

However, what about the danger posed by Big Business in the national economy, as well as in political, military, and social life? In his own book, *The New Language of Politics*, Safire writes of the military-industrial complex as follows:

> An increasingly powerful combination of forces that, left unchecked, would soon control the U.S. economy and foreign policy. Dwight Eisenhower, a military man whose friends were industrialists startled the nation with his farewell address on January 17, 1961, warning of the danger of military-industrial power ... Until WWII, Eisenhower said, the U.S. had no permanent armaments industry ... But the danger pointed out by Eisenhower was more subtle than militarism, or civilian control of the military ... These companies, through their economic impact on an area, had political power of their own that contributed to military appropriation decisions, building a vicious circle or "complex". That is how such entanglements of big corporations perpetuate their own highly organized special interests and interfere with government working in the public interest. On that account, it behooves America and Americans to propose effective measures that will break and abolish the reigning grip of those vested special interests.

Safire makes it clear that when he talks about Big Government he is "talking about the Federal Government." His text in this book elucidates the difficulties involved when one confronts the problem of the re-organization of the Federal Government, especially the Congress. As Safire notes, "That's not re-organization; that's revolution, in Washington, because the bureaucracy is pretty much run by the congressional staffs and when you talk about re-organization, that's cutting them. So the first thing the President does about this fine, high principled idea of re-organization, is a pragmatic thing, which is to say, 'I want the same authority (which is dodging the issue) that my predecessors have had.' By granting Authority, the legislature turns over to the Executive Branch its responsibilities and obligations . . . That's the way re-organization is being done." Such an approach, Safire properly affirms, is "dealing with the politics of the problem and not with the problem itself."

In reference to the federal investigations now underway into alleged Korean-CIA payoffs to legislators of about a million dollars a year, he said that about 50 congressmen were involved, mostly Democrats, over the past six years; and he predicted indictments will be forthcoming by fall.

In a question and answer period, he said that former Secretary of State, Henry Kissinger, with whom he was formerly friendly, is a gracious and lovable man; that "he has come to see himself as a chosen instrument of American freedom and that this megalomania was destructive of a good man." In reply to another question, Safire characterized organized labor in America as "probably the single strongest conservative force", far more than the Chamber of Commerce and the NAM; conservative not only in foreign affairs, high tariff, anti-free trade but also in anti-price control, anti-wage control, anti-government manipulation. The more that we have of government control of the economy, the less collective bargaining will be needed, and the less need there will be for labor unions.

L. William Seidman, born 53 years ago at Grand Rapids, Michigan, former consultant to the Republican Party in Washington and White House Economist, served the then Vice President Ford as Assistant for Administration and Public Affairs. After Ford became President, Mr. Seidman was appointed Assistant to the President for Economic Affairs. In that post he had many responsibilities, serving on energy resources councils, agricultural committees, councils on wage and price stability and other domestic councils while in addition serving as Executive Director of the Economic Policy Board established in 1974. In this latter capacity Seidman promptly and expeditiously organized the unique "Economic Summit Meeting," first of its kind in any country during which practitioners and theoreticians discussed the nation's economic problems and suggested diverse ways for their improvement.

Prior to his Federal Government Service, Bill Seidman was the managing partner of the International Certified Public Accounting firm bearing the Seidman name. He went to work for the family firm after he had won an A.B. Degree from Dartmouth College, where he majored in economics and was elected to Phi Beta Kappa. His LL.B. Degree was earned from the Harvard Law School; and his Master's Degree in Business Administration from the University of Michigan. For many years he has been a tax and budget advisor to Michigan governors. His interest in education prompted him to organize an influential group which founded a Michigan university, Valley State College, in 1963 which now has a student enrollment of nearly 8,000. Bill Seidman continues his association with Valley State College as chairman of the college's Board of Trustees. He is also a consultant and special advisor to the Aspen International Institute for Humanisitic Studies located in our nation's capitol. Very recently, Mr. Seidman has become Chief Executive of The Phelps Dodge Company, the world's second largest enterprise in mining copper and other valuable metals as well as marketing their related products.

Mr. Seidman titles his talk "Big Government and the International Economic Scene." As complex as domestic economics is, Mr. Seidman boldly ventures into the even greater complexity of the interrelationships among domestic "Big Government" and global economics. His are interesting, informed and timely comments of problems closely articulated and unified with regard to domestic and international economics, both intricate components of a single economic matrix. In this regard, he cites some pertinent major instances worthy of consideration. They include trade, commodities and the balance of trade and financial positions. Without offering any solutions, he gives us clearer understanding of the formidable economic complexities from the domestic-global aspect; and he predicts that global "free trade" will be more and more of the Russian American grain agreement variety and less "private sector Adam Smith-type free trade." He points out that this increased involvement of "Big Government" in the international trade scene may not be wholly negative. Particularly when balanced against such practices by multinational corporations as the shifting of capital and technology to those areas of the world where there are currently no minimum labor costs and work standards.

The success of OPEC in operating an effective price-fixing cartel in oil has encouraged the poor commodity exporting countries of the world to attempt to establish similar organizations to control such commodities as copper, aluminum, bananas or tea. Mr. Seidman sees such multi-national stabilization efforts as being of extremely limited effectiveness because of the unique position of oil as a rare commodity and the twin stumbling blocks of economic reality and political activity. Nevertheless he predicts that a complex system of governmental controls and a common trust fund will be established by a number of the poor commodity exporting countries in the short run.

The final area of international economic activity discussed by Mr. Seidman is the current severe imbalance of international trade. As he expressed it, "Never have so many borrowed so much, with such poor prospect of repayment." Largely the result ot the OPEC oil price increases, there is today a prospect of many countries being forced to default on their debt repayment which would result in a crippling of the world financial system. World economic interdependence has resulted in large debts between even adversary nations. He cites the Soviet Bloc's indebtedness to the world's industrial democracies of $30-40 billion which continues to grow at a rate of $10-12 billion a year. But the most serious problem is for nations to find the means of paying for the oil they need. For the wealthier nations this could mean less reliance on credit and lowering their standards of living through transfers of real wealth to the oil producers. This will require unpopular and politically difficult action. But for the less developed nations, Mr. Seidman sees no apparent practical solution. He predicts that this pressing imbalance of trade could become the "Vietnam" of the Carter administration. In this area government has seriously fallen behind the need for its regulatory presence. Each country is faced with taking an active role in determining its degree of dependence. He cites China and Japan as opposite examples of a government's active decision to seek either independence or dependence. The United States has allowed our policy of increased dependence to come about through default rather than decision. In order for us to move from a government of passive complexity to one of active efficiency the regulated private sector must teach the government how best to use its regulatory power beginning with the Congress of the United States.

The diverse views of "Big Government" presented by our three lecturers illustrate how complex and internationally inderdependent United States government is and how urgently important it is that it become an ever more efficient and competent regulator and policy maker. Their talks make it clear that for us to achieve this efficiency it is essential that the historical bond between the private and public sectors must be made even more secure, a means must be found to allow the administration to actually reorganize the bureaucratic maze perpetuated by congress, and the private citizen must accept the fact that "Big Government" is an integral part of today's reality and that indeed in such areas as international trade and finance yet another layer of "Big Government" may have to be created to forestall the ultimate collapse of the world financial system.

Acknowledgements

The Editor is again grateful to all who have participated in the continued success of the Lecture Series: to our benefactors, Mr. and Mrs. P. K. Seidman for their generous financial support and for P.K.'s devoted participation in the Coordinating Committee's detailed activities; to Memphis State University and President Billy M. Jones for officially sponsoring the M. L. Seidman Memorial Town Hall Lectures, which are held in the Fine Arts Complex; to Jerry N. Boone, Vice President for Academic Affairs, Memphis State University for his official and personal participation in the functions of the Coordinating Committee; to each guest lecturer and the University's staff members who introduced them; to the Coordinating Committee members, who assume their work eagerly and sedulously—their names are listed elsewhere in this book; to Dr. Festus Viser and Mr. Robert Garner, who respectively as Director and Assistant Director of the M. L. Seidman Town Hall Lectures, sustain a multiplicity of functions diligently and tactfully; to Mrs. Reva Cook for her expeditious publicity services; to Mr. Robert S. Rutherford who, as Director of Security at the University, safeguards the premises and the people attending the lectures; to Mrs. Barbara Lawhead for efficiently transcribing the lecture material to typescript, preliminary to final editing; and last but not least to the Memphis audience for enthusiastically attending the lectures.

"The Public and Private Sectors in the Fifth Kondratieff Upswing"

Lecture One

by W. W. Rostow

One basic duty of a social scientist is to be conscious of his prejudices and to make them clear to others. In discussing the role of the public and private sectors in our national life, I bring two prejudices or value judgments I should immediately share with you.

First, I believe in general that a private, competitive free enterprise system is intrinsically better than a system of socialism. It is more consistent with human freedom; it is generally, not always more efficient; and it has the great virtue of forcing the society to cut its losses when resources don't pay their way. Public enterprises have a considerable capacity to survive even when they are using resources inefficiently, as Britain and a good many other countries have demonstrated in recent times.

Second, unlike Milton Friedman,* I believe Adam

---

*Professor Friedman's attack on this passage from Adam Smith appears in a generally laudatory essay, *Adam Smith's Relevance for 1976*, Los Angeles: International Institute for Economic Research, Original Paper 5, December 1976, pp. 11-15.

Smith was right when he defined an area for public enterprise in these terms: "The duty of erecting and maintaining certain public works and certain public institutions which it can never be for the interest of any individual, or small group of individuals, to erect and maintain, because the profit could never repay the expense to any individual or small group of individuals, though it may frequently do much more than repay it to a great society."

The fact is that our great society has evolved, since the days when Alexander Hamilton won President Washington's backing, through partnership between the public and private sectors. The public sector not only created a setting of trade and financial policy within which private enterprise could flourish, it built the Cumberland Road and the Erie Canal; subsidized the long-distance rail lines; provided mass public education and then the agricultural and technological colleges which have proved so useful. It engaged the Corps of Engineers in massive public works programs of the kind envisaged by Adam Smith. It developed for large public purposes the potentialties of some of our rivers, yielding the TVA in this region, for example, and the lower Colorado River Authority in Central Texas. It leaned against monopolies or regulated them. In the wake of the Great Depression of the 1930's, it assumed responsibility for the level of employment, using, in part, the Federal Reserve System created earlier for other public purposes. It enlarged our educational systems, provided an approximation of equal opportunity for higher education, provided health services to our elderly citizens and the poor, and took other measures of equity an affluent people judged to be morally right. Moreover, many of our most important enterprises from rebuilding the centers of our cities to putting a man on the moon were accomplished by public-private collaboration almost too subtle and complex to describe, a kind of collaboration that rarely makes its way into the textbooks in economics or government.

Every one of these operations had its flaws and costs, as we are all aware. Since Hamilton jousted with Jefferson, there was always, and there remains, legitimate reason for debate at the margin concerning the appropriateness of one or another form of public intervention in the economy. Some were clearly disastrous, like the NRA during the New Deal and the fixing of the gas price in the 1950's. But I believe we were correct to build our society through a public-private partnership; and I believe we would be well advised to set aside the notion of a polar choice between the public and private sectors, accept the verdict of our history and that of other advanced industrial democracies, and go on from there, arguing policy case by case.

So much for my prejudices.

Against that background, my theme tonight is that the tasks of both our public and private sectors have radically changed in the past four years; and that the viability of our society in the future depends on our understanding that change and acting in new ways on both public and private levels.

Consider first the great worldwide boom of the 1950's and 1960's.

That expansion was unique in economic history. Never before had world production and trade expanded as fast. Never, since modern business cycles became part of economic life, had that expansion been so steady or marked by such low average levels of unemployment for so long a period. The boom of those two decades had two main sectoral pillars in the advanced industrial world: the diffusion of the automobile, durable consumer goods and the life of suburbia, with all their attendant technologies and massive secondary effects; and a sharp rise in outlays for certain public and private services which expand disproportionately in rich countries (notably, higher education, health services, and travel).

From 1951 to the closing months of 1972 the boom was conducted in a supportive environment of relatively declining prices of foodstuffs and raw materials, including energy. The price of electricity in the United States, for example, fell 41% relative to the general price level in those two decades. In the 1960's, the rate of increase of global demand for grain outpaced that of supply. This led to an enlargement of the number of grain deficit countries, a concentration of surpluses in the United States, Canada and Australia, as well as a drawing down of world grain reserves as a proportion of consumption. All this rendered the world market exceedingly vulnerable to a bad global harvest year like that of 1972, and the exercise by the Soviet Union of its bargaining power as a large importer. Similarly, the rate of increase of United States demand for oil outpaced the rate of increase in United States supply, leading to an increased dependence on oil imports from the Middle East and an end to the illusion that the United States was a reserve energy supplier. Oil production began its absolute decline in 1970-71. The process was exacerbated by United States natural gas policy, which blithely ignored the rapid decline in reserves. All this rendered the world market exceedingly vulnerable to the exercise in 1973 by the OPEC governments of their virtually monopolistic powers in the international oil market.

These price increases in grain and energy struck at the sectoral pillars of growth in the industrialized world in multiple ways. The rise in energy prices caused increased consumer outlays for energy (despite some economies) and reduced outlays for other goods and services. The upshot was a sharp decline during 1974 and 1975 in outlays for houses, automobiles and durable consumer goods which quickly reduced investment levels. The consequent recession was intensified by increased caution both among businessmen and consumers. Against this background, the second pillar of the great postwar boom (increased public and private outlays for certain services) was also weakened. Travel was constrained, for example, as were public outlays for education and other welfare services. In some cases, the latter may have been approaching a natural phase of deceleration after two decades of disproportionate expansion. But, in addition, as private real incomes stagnated or declined, a political revolt swept the industrial world against increased public outlays at the old rate. It was reflected in elections and the rhetoric of politicians from New Zealand and Australia to Britain and Sweden to New York and California. Without unemployment insurance and other income stabilizers we have created in the past forty years, a dangerously acute world depression might well have been set in motion.

Now we are in a slow and uncertain period of recovery; for we can no longer rely on the sectoral bases for growth of the 1950's and 1960's. The most optimistic projections suggest we shall still experience more than 7% average unemployment in 1977, accompanied by an inflation rate of over 5%. If this is a roughly correct forecast, we will have experienced four successive years of both high unemployment and acute, if somewhat diminished, inflation. The average unemployment level for the 1960's was 4.8%; the average rate of inflation, only 2.5%.

Before discussing the roles of public and private sectors in remedying this unwholesome situation, let me pull back the camera, as it were, and talk briefly as an economic historian.

This is the fifth time over the past two hundred years that a rise in the relative prices of basic commodities has occurred similar to the one which we have experienced since the end of 1972; and on each of the other four occasions it has been accompanied by manifestations similar to those we have experienced over the past four years: an accelerated general inflation, an extremely high range of interest rates, pressure on the real wages of industrial labor, pressure on those with relatively fixed incomes and shifts of income favorable to producers of food as well as energy. The other four parallel occasions occurred in the 1790's, the early 1850's, the second half of the 1890's, and the late 1930's. On each occasion, food and raw material prices after an initial sharp rise then fluctuated in a relatively high range for about a quarter-century. Approximately another quarter-century followed during which the trends reversed; that is, the prices of basic commodities were relatively cheap, as they were, for example, from 1951 to 1972. Each of these periods was, in an important sense, unique and the trends did not unfold smoothly; but the fact is that the

Seidman Lectures

world economy for almost two centuries has been subject to a rough and irregular pattern of long cycles in which periods of about 20 to 25 years of high relative prices for food and raw materials gave way to approximately equal phases of relatively cheap food and raw materials. This is, in my view, the fundamental characteristic of the long cycles associated with the name of the Russian economist, N. D. Kondratieff.*

I am not wedded to the notion that these cycles will continue in the future. But I would guess that the inexorable pressure of excessive population increase in the developing world, the tendency of the poor to spend increases in income disproportionately on food, the rising demand for grain-expensive proteins among the rich, and the high marginal cost of expanding the non-OPEC energy supply will persist for some time. Given these powerful and sustained forces operating on the prices of food, energy and raw material prices and the costs we shall have to incur to achieve and maintain clean air and water, I believe we are in for a long period when the prices of these basic inputs to the economy will remain relatively high. Indeed, I would guess that we shall only have a fifth Kondratieff downswing if and when we create a new, cheap (hopefully infinite and non-polluting) energy source. As we all know, energy is a critical factor not only in its own right but also because of its role in agriculture and the extraction of raw

---

*I analyze long cycles in "Kondratieff, Schumpeter, and Kuznets: Trend Periods Revisited," *Journal of Economic History*, Vol. 35, No. 4, December 1975, pp. 719-53. A full account of these cycles is included in Part Three of my forthcoming book *The World Economy: History and Prospect*, Austin: University of Texas Press.

materials and, potentially, in rendering economical the conversion of salt water into fresh water.

Down to 1914 the classic response to a Kondratieff upswing was to open new agricultural and raw material producing areas: the American West, Canada, Australia, Argentina, and the Ukraine. The great movements of international capital during this era were, in substantial part, induced by the price system, combined with new technologies of transport and production, to bring new supplies into the market and to restore balance in the world economy. In the fourth Kondratieff upswing (say, 1936-51), the diffusion of new agricultural technologies, rather than the opening of new physical frontiers, reestablished a tolerable balance in food production without much conscious government intervention; although in the field of energy the exploitation of Middle East oil after 1945 ranks with the opening up of the American West in agriculture a century earlier. But in the 1970's and beyond we confront the fifth Kondratieff upswing period in a setting quite different from that of the past. I wish we could, but we cannot realistically rely to the same extent on the automatic workings of the price system and private capital markets to restore and maintain balance. All over the world, in one way or another, policy toward resources is in the hands of governments or is strongly influenced by governments. At every stage in the effort to restore balance, therefore, public policy will be involved. We shall have to think and consciously act our way through the fifth Kondratieff upswing.

As we face this inescapable problem of policy making, the key lesson from history about Kondratieff upswings is exceedingly simple: to maintain an industrial society in the face of relatively expensive basic products, it is necessary to increase investment in ways which will expand the supply of those basic products or economize their use. The central operational fact about Kondratieff upswings is that the pattern of investment, the directions of investment, must change. As of 1977 the list of basic products demanding increased investment is longer and more complex than in the past when it was mainly grain or cotton that ran short. We evidently need to invest more in energy, energy conservation, and agriculture, here and abroad. If we succeed in reattaining high growth rates in the industrial world, we shall probably need to invest more in raw materials and their conservation. We shall certainly have to invest more to assure an adequate supply of water for irrigated agriculture in important areas of the United States, as well as to clean the water and air and maintain an agreeable physical environment. In the United States, it is quite probable that we shall have to put large investments into a cost-effective rehabilitation of our railway system and into mass transport in urban areas. Finally, we need a large increase in outlays directed to research and development in both the private and public sectors. We need more research and development for two reasons: first, because our rate of increase in productivity has been declining since the 1960's, in part because we have been allocating a reduced proportion of our national income to research and development; second, because research and development is going to be the equivalent, in our time and the time of our children, to the great open frontiers available to the world economy, to restore its balance, in the three pre-1914 Kondratieff upswings. A few frontiers there are: Alaska, the North

Sea, the seabeds, some parts of Australia and Canada. But basically, it is our ingenuity, expressed through science, invention, and innovation, which will have to see us through.

If I read correctly the lesson of history and if my view of our times is roughly accurate, the key task ahead is to bring about a massive increase in investment in energy and energy conservation; agricultural production; raw material production and conservation; water development; pollution control; research and development. And this will have to be done through the collaboration of the public and private sectors. As I said earlier, a public role is inescapable because, for good or ill, governments, here and abroad, are inextricably involved in policy towards energy, agriculture, raw materials, the environment, research and development. It is no longer a matter of throwing rail lines into an empty territory and letting private enterprise and the flow of immigrants do the rest.

But the role of private enterprise remains critical. Indeed, the first duty of public policy is to set a framework within which private enterprise can do a maximum of the job. For example, it is urgent that we settle on a stable energy price policy and settle the environmental rules of the game so that private enterprise can carry the bulk of the burden of expanding energy production and increasing energy conservation. Public policy could also help by offering tax incentives to insulate houses and to install solar energy in the limited but important range where solar energy is now cost-effective. Tax incentives and other forms of indirect public aid could lead private enterprise to undertake (notably in energy) tasks otherwise too large or too risky. We might also consider increased incentives to expand private research and development. This should include relevant research in the universities as well as in the business community. But in certain limited areas, the government will have residual direct responsibilities; for example, in water development and water cleaning projects; in rehabilitating now sub-marginal agricultural land; in transport; and in some aspects of research and development.

On the public side, I believe we shall require something like the old RFC: the Reconstruction Finance Corporation, created by President Hoover, was used effectively in both peace and war by President Franklin Roosevelt; run at a profit by Jesse Jones on behalf of the taxpayer. We should also consider, in both the federal and state budgets, separating out the investment components from other outlays less directly productive.

But, above all, we need the federal government, in consultation with business and labor—and in consultation with state governments as well—to take stock of our investment requirements as a nation over, say, the next ten years. That assessment, engaging under central direction all the relevant government departments and agencies in Washington, should lead to estimates of what we need to do to bring our economy back to balance and to assure its continued high productivity. I am confident that the scale of required productive investment would emerge as so large that we would have to think in terms of priorities. Despite our high unemployment and idle industrial capacity, I believe we would face a capital shortage, in the sense that we would come to understand that we have more to do than we can do all at once, and we should certainly not be running our industrial system at 80% capacity.

This rough assessment of investment needs and priorities would also tell us, I believe, something else: we need every man and woman we can get in the working force. It would tell us that there is no reason whatsoever that we should settle for 7% unemployment. It would tell us that, despite all the familiar difficulties, we have to find a way to bring into productive steady work the great idle or partially unemployed pools of labor in the heart of the northern cities and in the rural south. It is our lack of imagination and initiative which makes us regard these people as a sad social burden rather than a major potential asset of the nation.

My message to my friends in Washington, then, is this: We shall never get back to sustained full employment and we shall never deal successfully with the distortions of the fifth Kondratieff upswing unless we develop a public-private investment program something like the one I have described. That is the missing element in our thought and policy; although the proposal to put some of the unemployed to work on resource conservation and transport tasks is a limited step in the right direction. But cutting taxes a little, making a big federal deficit a bit bigger, expanding public service jobs which do not relate to the nation's priority tasks, easing our monetary policy a little—all this will expand the economy to some extent, for a while; but these actions will not put the economy on a path of sustained rapid growth and structural adjustment. We need an investment-based phase of rapid growth in an environment of high energy prices to take the place of the consumption-oriented phase of rapid growth—based on cheap energy prices—which we enjoyed in the 1950's and 1960's.

To achieve that result, we need new methods of public-private cooperation and a new spirit of public-private cooperation in the national interest. I believe President Carter is in an admirable position to create those methods and evoke the new spirit.

In making these recommendations I claim no greater wisdom. But I have been, all my mature life, an historian as well as an economist. I am, if you like, a child of the past two centuries. Most modern economists, whether conservative or liberal, are children of the 1930's.

To have been formed as an economist by the 1930's has profound implications; for it was then that what we call the Keynesian Revolution was born—a revolution so pervasive that even President Nixon announced himself a Keynesian, although at precisely the time that Keynes' doctrines of the 1930's were becoming substantially misleading.

Keynes, like many of his contemporaries, was focused on one great problem: How should unemployment, which was very high in the Western world, be reduced? He perceived that, despite high unemployment, money wage rates did not fall enough, to clear the market, as classical economic analysis would decree. Therefore, he focused on measures to increase the level of effective demand through government deficit spending and lowered interest rates. He said it didn't matter if men were put to work digging holes in he ground and filling them up so long as they were working, being paid, and spending what they earned. He also counseled that we should not worry about what economists call long period factors: the expansion of plant, for example, or the introduction of new technologies, or the supply of food, energy, and raw materials. He justified this indifference in long period factors with his famous dictum: "In the long run we are all dead." In the 1930's, food and raw materials were cheap, so cheap, in fact, that Britain's export customers, who produced them, couldn't buy British products. British unemployment was concentrated in its export industries. Keynes had no immediate reason to worry about the long run availability of basic products. Although Keynes' view is understandable as a response to the 1930's, it is a quite inappropriate doctrine for a time when long period factors press in on us every day, which we will ignore only at great and increasing cost.

The theoretical system that emerged from the Keynesian Revolution was, then, almost wholly focused on the problem of effective demand. The supply side of the equation is either introduced abstractly and arbitrarily or it is assumed that supply will take care of itself, if only demand is high enough.

This is not a sufficient theoretical system for an economic historian. An historian has to deal with the coming in of new technologies and industries: cotton textiles, the steam engine, railroads, steel, and all the rest. He must deal with periods of shortage and abundance of food and cotton, timber, coal, and oil. To do my job as an economic historian, I had to create a dynamic system that dealt with supply as well as demand. I am, therefore, a good deal more at home in the fifth Kondratieff upswing than are most of my professional colleagues and friends.

If you look closely at the arguments of more conventional economists their debate comes to rest on two issues: first, should one try to manipulate effective demand through monetary or through fiscal policy? Second, what is the correct trade-off between the rate of inflation and the rate of unemployment? In effect, the latter issue was at the heart of the economic debate between President Ford and Governor Carter during the recent campaign. The major neo-Keynesian economists, Republican and Democratic, live in a world where there is no coherent place for wheat or meat, gas, oil, or coal, research and development. They think about investment simply in terms of its aggregate volume and how it will affect the level of effective demand. They become distinctly uneasy when one suggests the need to change the directions of investment.

These neo-Keynesian habits of thought dig deep into our politics; for politicians have to rely on economists whether they wish to or not. That is why President Ford could not break out of stagflation and why President Carter's first moves to revive the economy were so conventional and incomplete. Before we're fully squared away to deal with the fifth Kondratieff upswing, we may need an intellectual revolution as profound as the Keynesian Revolution itself.

This brings me to inflation, about which I can only comment briefly tonight.

There are three kinds of inflation. Demand-pull inflation occurs when labor is fully employed and industrial capacity is being fully used. Obviously we don't have that kind of inflation now. Then there is raw materials push inflation when the prices of basic commodities rise sharply because of changes on the supply side. That occured in 1972-74; then the pressure eased in the face of a levelling off of energy prices, good harvests, and the effects of recession on raw material prices. Finally, there is wage-push inflation, when money wages rise faster than our average increase in productivity. Despite severe chronic unemployment, we have been steadily experiencing wage-push inflation. In 1976, for example, money wages increased about 8%; average productivity, about 3%. The gap between money wage and productivity increases is expected to continue. That is primarily why more than 5% inflation is predicted for 1977.

I do not underestimate the difficulties that democratic societies face in bringing wage-push inflation under control. To control wage-push inflation requires that labor accept money wage increases geared to the average increase in the nation's productivity. The economic history of the past thirty years is littered with efforts by democratic governments to implement wage restraint policies that worked, at best, for relatively short periods of time. On the other hand, I do not believe we should accept defeat and go on living with inflation. First, we know that there is a deep anxiety in our society concerning inflation. In public opinion polls it is usually judged as a problem of higher priority than unemployment. Thus, there is a political base for dealing with inflation if we can generate the political statesmanship. Second, I am convinced that labor leaders would be prepared for sustained wage restraint if we could find credible ways to guarantee two conditions: (1) that no labor leader or group of workers lose or gain significantly relative to any other, and (2) that wage discipline not result in a disproportionate increase in distributed profits. Given the institutional structure of our unions and political life, these are not easy criteria to meet; but they are by no means impossible. What we require is a formula to be worked out between labor and business that is backed by the full commitment of the Executive Branch and Congress; a program designed to last at least five years. We need a period of this length to allow an initial phase of equity adjustment of wage rates negotiated at different times in the past and, after that, a long enough period to alter expectations. A good deal of inflationary pressure arises because business and labor expect inflation; hedge against it; and bring about what they fear. We are like a dog chasing his tail.

I believe, moreover, that a good setting within which to try to deal with wage-push inflation is a time in which, in any case, we as a national community ought to be cooperating to deal with problems of energy, food, and the environment which have recently marched to the center of the stage.

What our experience of recent years has proved is that there is no effective and realistic way to halt wage-push inflation except by an act of cooperation embracing the whole national community. Whatever the difficulties, I believe that in the United States and other democracies we must try to learn how to work together to this end; for inflation corrodes our provisions for the future, our private institutions, our tax structure, and it distorts the whole process of investment.

Now, a final word, returning to the central theme of private enterprise. As I said at the beginning, for deep and abiding reasons, I prefer private to public enterprise. We are a society whose best performance requires many centers of responsibility, initiative, and decision.

That proposition holds for our economy, but also for our intellectual life, our social life, and our politics.

But private enterprise must earn its way. It must do its job. It must be enterprising, risk-taking, and vigorous. Here we have a problem about which I can talk bluntly since I speak as a teacher and a citizen, tied neither to private enterprise nor to politics. Private enterprise in our country was frightened by a phase in the Congress when private enterprise was wrongly used as a scapegoat in energy matters and rightly questioned about some of its practices in politics at home and bribery overseas.

All this made the private business community tend to pull in its horns and go defensive. I don't know what concerned me more: the demagoguery of some members of the Congress or the excessive reaction of some of our business leaders. Some aspects of this phase of supercaution were helpful; for example, the proportion of short-term indebtedness of corporations has been substantially reduced. And now, with profits rising, corporate balance sheets look a good deal better. Moreover, the Congress will be, I believe, more thoughtful and mature on energy policy this term than in the last; and having exposed some of the mistakes made by private enterprise, I don't believe Congress is in a mood for an indefinitely prolonged witch hunt.

Against this background, I sense that now is the time for private enterprise to perform in a more enterprising way. Profits should be ploughed back at a higher rate into productive investment. Research and development outlays should be increased. Private enterprise should be willing to enter a sustained dialogue with government and labor about what it can do in the critical

Seidman Lectures

sectors which must expand if our economy is to have a sound foundation; and what business can do to make it easier for labor to accept wage restraints geared to productivity increases. It is time for private enterprise to get moving again with confidence.

There is a sense in which we were all a little spoiled in the 1950's and 1960's. In part, it was because the relative prices of energy, food, and raw materials were low. In part, it was because it is not difficult for a private enterprise system to manufacture and diffuse automobiles, durable consumer goods, and suburban houses; and, with a rising tax base, it is not difficult for legislators—in Washington and in the state capitals—to vote more money for schools, hospitals, and social services. It was not wise but it is understandable that prophets should appear in the 1960's proclaiming that affluence was automatic, assured, and could be taken for granted. It was also understandable that part of a generation of the white affluent young believed those prophets and searched for values and a way of life beyond material affluence. Some of the results of all this were costly; some generated an idealism we still need. Now we are back in a world where, evidently, our affluence is not assured; where hard choices have to be made; where old-fashioned virtues, like hard work and ingenuity, are needed, as well as a determination to improve the quality of our society.

One of my themes tonight is, simply, then, that among the old-fashioned virtues we must revive is enterprise in our private enterprise system. The agenda ahead is somewhat different than that which business confronted in the 1950's and 1960's. It is also different for government and politics than the agenda of the previous generation. But, if we as a national community can develop a common vision of where we have come from, where we are, what we must do together to maintain and develop our society, I have no doubt a fruitful new phase in the old public-private partnership is within our grasp.

"Big Government"

Lecture Two

by William Safire

The topic tonight, "Big Government," is dear to my heart because I've been inveighing against it for many years. I appreciate too the fact that the gentleman who introduced me didn't leap over the name "Nixon." Usually I'm introduced clearly as "speech writer in the White House in the years (there follows a muffled rumble)" and I wear this tie clasp proudly, given me then by the President of the United States. I never wore it in the White House because I thought it was kind of apple-polishing to do that. But now that nobody will be caught dead with it, I'm happy to wear it. I don't run away from my service in those years. I can take a ribbing on it. I heard a good joke just the other day about the presidency. A good comedian in New York said that "Two hundred years ago we had George Washington. He never told a lie. Today we have Jimmy Carter. He never tells a lie. With Nixon, we had a little relief."

I got out of the White House and joined *The New York Times* in early '73. I remember very well the day I left. I cleaned out my desk in the Executive Office Building across the street from the White House, got ready to leave, walked down the hall and I saw two Secret Service men standing outside the hideaway office that Mr. Nixon had in the EOB as we called it. I thought to myself, "That means that he's in there and I'm just walking by now—should I poke my head in and say goodby?" The pretty receptionist outside waved and gave me the high-sign as if to say, "You want to go in?" I thought about it for a second and realized that I'd already written the letter of resignation, and I'd already written his letter back to me saying what a great job I'd done. These are among the fringe benefits you get as a ghost-writer in the White House and I didn't like the awkward situation, so I kept walking on out into the sunshine. I found out years later that was March 21, 1973, 4:00 o'clock in the afternoon, and that very monent, in that office, the President and John Dean and Bob Haldeman were talking about "the cancer on the Presidency." Had I walked into the room, as I had a right to do, I would have been on the tape, and the President might have said, "Bill, sit down, listen to this." I might not, five seconds later, have leaped to my feet saying, "But it would be wrong," had I not done that, I would not be a columnist now for *The New York Times*.

So time and chance happen to us all and I don't stand around, polishing my halo, as one of those who came through those years and the hysteria that followed with any glee. I do remember, though, that in terms of big government there's a bureaucratic mind-set that afflicts everyone. It's a bad thing. It's a necessary concommitant to big government. I remember I ws writing a Vietnam cease-fire speech and I'd received some information from Henry Kissinger who was then a friend of mine. This was before I found out that he was tapping my telephone, and one of the memoranda had a intriguing and zippy thing across the top. It said, "Top Secret, No Dis, Sensitive, President's Eyes Only." I thought that it had a good ring to it so I put a page in my typewriter and started writing the draft of the President's speech. Just to give myself an extra sense of the dramatic, I wrote across the top, "Top Secret, No Dis, Sensitive, Exclusively President's Eyes Only", which inspired me and I wrote a zingy speech and sent it on in and waited for the President's reaction. For the first time, I didn't get any reaction at all. He didn't send the draft speech back with those little chicken scratchings all over it. I waited a couple of days and I called up the Office of the President and the secretary said, "I'm sorry but we can't let you have that," and I said, "But I need the speech back so that I can write a second draft," and the answer was, "Well, the problem is you're not cleared for "Top Secret, Sensitive, No Dis." You people laugh, but that's the way it was.

Now when we talk about that kind of mind-set and big government, i.e. when you have to deal with it whether you're a columnist or a White House aide, when you have to deal with this monolith and you come to Washington and you think you can move it around, they first tell you the story of the Bureau of Indian Affairs. As you know, the number of American Indians have not been growing anywhere near as fast as the number of American Bureaucrats, and when you go into the Bureau of Indian Affairs there is this vast panoply of gray desks, for miles it seems, with men and women working at those desks. The story is told of the

White House aide who walked in and saw everybody busily working away except for one man who was sobbing at his desk and walked up to him and said, "Is there something I can do? Has something terrible happened?" and the man said, "Yes. My Indian died."

Now, as to the growth of government. Government in 1900 consumed about 8% of our taxes; employed about 4% of our labor force. Thirty years later in the heyday of Herbert Hoover, taxes were up to about 11% of the GNP and 6% of the labor force worked for the government. A year ago, taxes were up to 33% at all levels; and 15% of the American labor force worked for state, federal or local government. If we take that curve and project it, at the current rate of growth, by the year 2000, 50% of the GNP will be paid in taxes, and 25% of the people in the labor force will be working for government.

Now, that's the welfare state. That's a strangulated economy and that, I think, is something that should alarm every American, Democrat, Republican, Liberal or Conservative. As it happens I'm a Conservative. I'm sure of that. I can tell it every morning. I'm not always right but I'm always certain and one of the things I'm certain of is that this steady growth of government is pernicious and saps not only the American spirit but American business and the ability to start something. In this land of entrepreneurs, it has become murder to get anything started, to get any product launched. Everybody remembers Thalidamide and its terrible results, and now make certain that every product is checked out four ways. Every new company that is launched has to go through all kinds of procedures. Most enterprises, even ones of great pitch and moment, are "sent awry" in

Hamlet's words. And so it's just not a grim-faced old fogey, rightwinger, mumbling, "The Bureaucrats have taken over!" The sophisicates, too, recognize that Bureaucrat is a political word. A bureaucrat is a Democrat in a job a Republican wants, and vice versa. Yet, from the figures I've just given you, you can see that we're not just on a treadmill to oblivion, but on a steadily accelerating process and that something has to be done.

Now, we have Jimmy Carter in office and he has pledged to re-organize the Federal government and created the impression that through good management he will be able to stop the growth of government, and prevent the government from taking over. That was the impression that Mr. Nixon suggested as well. I don't care how you feel about Mr. Nixon on a variety of topics, but when it came to re-organization, he was pretty good at it and he had some good ideas on it. Whenever anybody says we ought to re-organize the Federal government, six task forces are gotten together and they turn to the Bureau of the Budget, which is now called the Office of Management and Budget, and say, "what have you got on re-organization?" and then they come up with what appears to be new material which is the older Hoover Commission stuff, dusted off, which is a perfectly good, sensible re-organization plan, modern, streamlined, but it has never been made real. The Hoover Commission in the Truman-Eisenhower Period came forth with it, the Nixon Men, good, bad, and indifferent, proposed it, and now the Carter Men are coming forth with it. It sounds good. It is good. The question is, "How much of it can get done?" And the one thing that disturbed me was, even in the campaign, when Jimmy Carter was anxious to show how he would really re-organize the government and save the taxpayers money, when it came to meeting with the Federal Employees Union, he assured them that no union member would lose his job as a result of federal government re-organization. Well, that was interesting. So everything will have to be done through attrition and in thirty years the growth of government can be stopped. I hope we haven't elected Jimmy Carter for that long. But that was a hint of suspicion. There are those of us who remember our little battle against the tea-tasters. There was, I should say, there is, a panel of tea-tasters that costs about $100,000 a year. Not a big deal. I remember I used that in the lead of a speech, saying, "We've got to sweep out this kind of stuff and reform the government and streamline and re-organize this archaic thing." Everybody laughed. David Brinkley went on television and told about the tea-tasters but we couldn't get them stopped. They're still there sipping tea, basically because the Congress wouldn't have any reform.

The reason that the Congress resists reform is that when you talk about re-organizing Big Government, which is the Legislative Branch, and I should say when I'm talking about Big Government I'm talking about the Federal Government. But you must realize that the State and Local Government has grown just as fast as the Federal Government. I think, as fast if not faster, so this is not a Washington-only problem. But let's take Washington because everybody likes to do that. You have a problem of re-organizing the Congress. You're going to say, "Good sense says we ought to take a particular function out of the Department of Labor and put it together with another function at the Department of Agriculture; and break the Department of Interior up into a Department of Natural Resources." It makes good sense and you organize things by missions rather than by titles. If you do that, you're also saying, "Well you're going to have to change the House Committee on Agriculture and to change the way the Senate operates on the Interior Committees. You're going to have to lose some seniority here and shake up some congressional staffs there." Now you're cutting close to the bone. That's not re-organization; that's revolution, in Washington, because the bureaucracy is pretty much run by the congressional staffs and when you talk about re-organization, that's cutting them.

So the first thing the President does, about this fine, high principled idea of re-organization, is a pragmatic thing, which is to say, "I want the same authority (which is dodging the issue) that my predecessors have had."

By granting Authority, the legislature turns over to the Executive Branch its responsibilities and obligations. For example, in the case of the pay raise for Congressmen. Instead of voting for their own pay raise which they have to justify to voters at home, they've got it rigged now where the President recommends it and unless the Congress votes against it and vigorously objects, it goes through. So it becomes law and a Congressman can come home and say, "I never voted for a pay raise." That's the way re-organization is being done. One lone kind of ornery Congressman, Jack Brooks of Texas, is saying, "Hey, I'm for good government operations, but why don't we vote it up and down instead of having this business of the President to propose something and unless the Congress objects, it goes through. Let the President propose something and let the Congress vote on it." Well, Congressman Brooks is being snickered at as a pleasant old curmudgeon, touting the

Constitution at a time when we're talking about modernization. So, he will be shunted aside and President Carter I think will be able to get some re-organization plans, like the one I mentioned, like an Energy Department or a Department of Human Resources and, cosmetically, I think you'll see some action, but I think they're approaching it in a fairly unprincipled way, a wrong way. I think its dealing with the politics of the problem and not with the problem itself.

How is President Carter doing in Washington? In a public relations sense I think he's doing fine. Never forget you're dealing with power structures and in talking about re-organizing the government, if the President has enough power, enough public support, and if the Congress has a diminution of public support and gets in trouble, then you have a possibility of real reform. If, however, those two things don't come to pass, you won't have substantial reform.

On the presidential side of the ledger, what happens after a close selection is that your President . . . if he gets in by 51 to 47% as Mr. Carter did, he'll gain 10% from people who'll lie about how they voted, so that's 60-40. That's pretty good. Then from a sense of momentum, a fact that he really is President, he goes on with "dial-a-prexy" phone calls, which are good, but which if a Republican did, would be denounced as Madison Avenue image-building, is instead "communication with the people." The "fireside chat" was an excellent idea. He handled that very well I thought. He's going over the head of the cynical back-biting columnists and commentators, sensation-seekers as Eisenhower used to call them, us. Occasionally you will hear me refer to the media. When I talk about the media, I'm against them; when I talk about the press, I'm for them. *The Commercial Appeal* is the press.

So what Carter has going for him is a rise now in his popularity. I think it will continue throughout the Spring but he's riding for a fall because what he's doing, in my opinion, and again this is an opinion, is he's being a "popularist". Not a "populist", a "popularist". He's trying to make as many friends as he can, taking a fairly middle position on economic policy, changes in the budget were minimal, and trying to make everybody happy on the foreign side. I'll come back to that or answer questions about that later if you like. Meanwhile what's going on in Washington and what's frightening the devil out of all Washingtonians is a burgeoning Watergate-type scandal which is now under the surface and beginning to bubble up.

Remember I said he needs two things in order to really reform. One is an increase in his own power and prestige and the other is that the Congressmen feel they are faced with a big problem. The problem that's bubbling in Washington now is that about 10% of the House of Representatives faces the possibility of indictment. The Korean-CIA scandal, which has not really been impressed on the public mind, is growing. The K-CIA for about six years, paid off, illegally, about a million dollars a year to U.S. Congressman, mainly Democratic members of the House. I insist that I would say this even if it were mainly Republicans. You can believe that or not. But the fact is this is what's happening and it is a scandal. Six million bucks may not be lot of money to most people but it adds up. A great many holier-than-thou, somewhat hypocritical men, who were talking about how the system works not too long ago, are worried that the system is liable to work on them. What has happened is that Tongsun Park, as you may recall, was sort of the middleman in these payments and had a great many of the members of the House of Representatives beholden to him and paid them off, sometimes through foundations. He's now in London and he's resisting extradition. Meanwhile, there was started about eight months ago, an investigation by the Justice Department. There was a Grand Jury, similar to the Watergate Grand Jury, taking testimony, every day, in secret. In comes the new attorney general, Griffen Bell and the first thing he tells the Grand Jury is, "Fish or cut bait. I mean you've been playing around with this for six or eight months. Either get an indictment, or drop the case." Well, that pleased some of the congressmen in the House who were anxious for the case to be given a deadline, but it did not please a lot of the members of the Justice Department in the middle levels and the lower levels, who felt that the Justice Department here, again, is on trial, the way it was in the Watergate Case (and it didn't do too well in the Watergate Case). So there is an institutional feeling at the Justice Department to follow this through.

Meanwhile, while this case is either being pursued or covered up, as the case may be in Justice, the House Ethics Committee is going to have to grapple with it and in the Senate this particular venality, to my knowledge, has not reached the Senate Select Committee on Intelligence. The most important word in Washington now is this word "select". That means that it is not a Democratic-dominated committee; it's a half and half committee, with a fairly objective staff. It has on it Senator Howard Baker, Minority Leader and he's determined to get this whole story. He hasn't been leaking. He has been in touch, I know, with Chairman Flint of the House Ethics Committee and he has said publicly there is a possibility of these forty or fifty Congressmen being in trouble. When the House Ethics Committee Chairman said, "Who do you mean?" just the other day (this hasn't come out yet, to my knowledge, but hang on and read my column soon). Senator Baker said, "We are studying this matter in the Select Committee and the relationship between the KCIA and the CIA and any collateral information we develop about Congressmen we'll be glad to send you."

So taking everything together, what you see now is a scandal in its kind of nascent, embryonic form, but a big one. Not as big as Watergate because forty or fifty Congressmen are not as interesting as a President but 'tis enough, 'twill do. It's a substantial scandal.

Now, how will this affect American politics? Well a lot of people will say, "Aah, they're all a bunch of crooks." That's the wrong thing to say. The fascinating thing is that as a result of the increase in the popularity of the president and the fear that's stalking the House, you may have a possibility of real reform of governmental structures, and this possibility will last a year, tops. If you can't get the reform accomplished this year, it's not going to happen. This is the only time a manager can come in, shake things up and accomplish reform. People in Washington come in, they don't know the obstacles, so they try, blunder on ahead and lots of times they sort of barrel the obstacles out of the way. It's a strange thing. It's a phenomenon. But after a year or so, you get to know the people, you develop some connective tissue, you start making certain compromises that are the lifeblood of Washington, and then suddenly reform and reorganization and cutting costs cease to become as important as delivering services to the people who are carrying on the grand traditions of the New Deal or whatever.

So I think the strange, not cancer on the Presidency, the strange venality in the House. if exploited properly by honest men, can redound to the benefit of people who believe in a slowing of the growth of Big Government. It can be a good thing. Symbols are not all but Jimmy Carter understands symbols. The business of the limousines in the White House. Brilliant! I mean it costs nothing to say to a couple of dozen guys, "Don't get driven to and from your house by a White House car." Now they made a big deal of that. Everybody hates to see somebody driven to work, unless it's you. So this was a great symbol. Two days later he made a mailing, a direct mail appeal to thousands of people, using the franking privilege on "What do you think of our energy program?" It was blatant political advertising in my book. It cost more than any kind of saving he could have possibly gotten from all the taking the guys to and from the White House. President Carter understands that. He's good at it, he's a good politician. Hats off to him for it. I don't think it's going to last too long. I think you can only do this the first year. So the honeymoon will last for awhile. It will be exploited well. I think the Big Government issue, which is his issue, and anti-Washington feeling, which is real, will be nicely exploited. But I think the feeling Americans have that the time finally has come for a taxpayers' revolt, for an understanding that alienation does exist among people who can't really get the grip on the national government or can't really stop

Seidman Lectures

the government from getting steadily bigger and bigger. I think this is going to reach out. This afternoon I was talking to the Memphis Economics Club, a group of distinguished community leaders and business leaders and academics. I was pontificating something about economic affairs and they were lapping it up in a camaraderie of power. After it was all over and I finished my speech and everybody applauded and we all shook hands, I started to go. A waitress came in and looked around at all these Big Shots, myself included, and said, "Who's going to sign the check?" Oh, I thought that was wonderful because that symbolized to me what's going on in Washington now. Who is going to sign the check? Nobody's been signing the check. We've been thinking in terms of federal dollars versus state dollars. They're not federal dollars, they're our dollars, they're taxpayers' dollars. And they've gotten wings on them and there've been not enough people to come in and say, "Who's going to sign the check?" and demand accountability. I think there's this need. The time is right now. If President Carter presses it and uses his growing power and the growing weakness of the House, he could conceivably make some impact on Big Government. If he misses this chance, comes the next budget and the next year, he'll never have a chance again. So, even Conservatives are rooting for Jimmy Carter to do the thing that he promised to do and if it results in his being more popular, we're just going to have to grin and bear it. Now I'm available for questions on any subject at all because one of the requirements for a columnist is to have a firmly considered opinion on everything.

"Big Government and the International Economic Scene"

Lecture Three

by L. William Seidman

It is a particular honor to be able to participate in these M.L. Seidman Lectures because M.L. was my esteemed uncle and first employer. He was a man of talent—and, as I soon found, he had a hand of steel in velvet glove.

I am also particularly pleased to be able to pay tribute to P.K. Seidman, my favorite uncle, who is the sponsor of this series among many other good works.

During my years working in the White House, hardly a week went by that I didn't receive a bit of solid advice from P.K. on economics, foreign relations, or energy. He seemed to feel that we, in the battle, weren't able to differentiate the forest from the trees. He said we didn't realize how inefficient big government was.

Hopefully, we will be able to do better than Big Government as we emphasize and *review* the international economic scene. The view is not entirely pleasant having to do with such items as questionable payments, boycotts, deficits, cartels, countervailing duties, and floating rates that don't float. The study of governance in international economics is like doing battle with an ancient Hydra—as soon as you slice off the head, two more grow in its place.

I note that *Time* magazine quotes Henry Kissinger as indicating that one reason for today's problems was a lack of competence of the Ford administration's people in international economics. If he made such a statement, it is one of startling modesty on the part of the great Henry, though it could be true in his case. But it is, I feel, basically untrue with respect to Simon, and Greenspan, and hopefully, yes, even *Bill Seidman*.

The fast growing and increasingly complex role of big government in international economics has even become the subject of a best selling novel, *The Crash of 1979*. The theme of this fiction piece is a domestic economic collapse brought on by world economic conditions. They are, uncontrolled, and, to some extent, the ones we will be reviewing tonight. Who could have predicted that exchange rates, petrodollars, tariffs and trade balances would replace the KGB, the Jackal and the CIA as subjects for a best seller? Still, the story of an economic crash in the US, caused by world economic conditions, contains enough fact to lend credence to the view that international economic activity has become very important to the operation of every business, whether in Duluth, Dallas, Memphis, Mobile, Grand Rapids, or New York.

For better or worse, international economic activity will affect the operation of businesses, large and small, inland and coastal, exporters, importers and "domestic only" operators. International economic interrelatedness adds to the complexity of management problems, whether in government or in the private sector.

In fact, in the Ford administration, both international and domestic policy were handled by one board, the Economic Policy Board (note the word "board"), of which I was privileged to be the Executive Director. This was the first time that US domestic and international economic policy were assigned to the same unit. We designed this arrangement because it had become quite clear that interrelatedness of international and domestic policy required that they be considered together. Previously, the complex relationship between domestic and international economics was confronted by the one person hired by the people to direct his attention to both areas—The President of the U.S.

It is interesting to note that, after some attempts to alter the facade, the Carter administration is following the same program, but with a brand new name—The Economic Policy Group.

A quick review of just how big international economic transactions have become:

- Total world trade: over $1 trillion since last year
    - US Exports: $115 billion
    - US Imports: $129 billion
- European Community:
    - Exports: $399 billion
    - Imports: $439 billion
- Communist Countries:
    - Exports: $ 93 billion
    - Imports: $102 billion
- US Assets Abroad: (1975) $304 billion
- Foreign Assets in US: $210 billion

—The US is dependent for 100 percent of its raw rubber, 84 percent of its aluminum, 40 percent of its oil.

—Japan is dependent for 100 percent of its rubber, 100 percent of its aluminum and 99.2 percent of its oil.

Now, we have heard the complaints about our big domestic US Government, and I subscribe to some of them. Yet a more pressing aspect of governance—big or nonexistant—relates to government of the international economic scene. Here also there are some important and immediate problems that may need action even before action is taken in our domestic problem areas. I talk about it for two reasons:

1. Big government is coming on the international scene.
2. In many areas it is needed, and promptly.

Three interrelated areas of international economic activity are of special interest and concern at this time. Together they may give a fairly accurate view of conditions and trends in the international scene. They are:

(1) Trade
(2) Commodities
(3) Balance of trade and financial positions

I like to have a little quotation for each of the sections I discuss to give an indication of what's to come. My first quote is from that ultimate marketeer and conservative, the former Secretary of the Treasury William Simon, who said,

> I consider Adam Smith's Invisible Hand to be an unwarranted interference in the operation of the free market.

Ever since Adam Smith, free trade in the private sector has been a key objective of enlightened and liberal world leadership. Presumably, the trade war of the thirties and the benefits of the Kennedy round of tariff reductions, have convinced all "right thinking" statesmen that freer and increased trade benefits the world's economies by each doing his own things, thus benefiting society as though being guided by an unseen hand. The new interdependence of economies which such trade brings is considered desirable. This view was upheld by the leadership of the world's industrial democracies at their economic summit meetings in Rambouillet and Puerto Rico. It is practically certain that such a statement will be the easy part to compose for those who write the communique for the upcoming Summit III in London in May. In the interim between Summit II and Summit III, and during the worst of the recent recession, there was a surprising lack of effective demand for trade barriers to "protect" jobs at home. To this point, there has been less slippage by free traders than expected, but that is about all one can say in looking for improved free trade conditions.

The Tokyo round of the GATT negotiations in Geneva so far, has produced little that can support hope for freer trade. Our US legislation, the Trade Act of 1974, set up a system which continued to assure pressure for protection. That Act was hailed as a step forward in promoting trade, and in many ways it gave the President important additional latitude to remove trade barriers and tariffs at home. But, through the international trade commission, it also gave industries "harmed" by trade, the right to a finding of such harm and a remedy based on quotas, tariffs, or subsidies.

More importantly, it gives the injured industry a Congressional override if the President does not follow the ITC Recommendation.

It is axiomatic that successful trade activities are going to harm some industries in the importing country, and ultimately put some of them out of business. The current shoe controversy is an example. The Trade commission has found harm to the US shoe industry and prescribed a remedy of quotas. The President has set aside the ruling and asked for voluntary quotas by exporters. Congress will have a chance to override his decision if voluntary quotas cannot be negotiated. But even "voluntary quotas" are hardly a vote of confidence in the future of free trade.

There are other clouds on the horizon for free traders. Methods of trade between Communist nonmarket economies and a free economy do not lend themselves to the old example of free trade. The 1975 Russian US grain deal is more likely to provide the pattern for the future than free private sector trade activities. World commodities, agreements, OPEC-type cartels and income transfers by way of North-South economic activity, all look to less, rather than more, freedom in international trading relations.

Everything from countervailing duties on Japanese TV's to Russian American grain agreements, points to more government and less freedom, not necessarily less, trade, but less private sector Adam Smith-type free trade.

The question arises whether these new limitations on trade are necessarily all adverse. Here are some factors to be considered: Non-market countries can use the private sector of market countries to their advantage unless government intervenes. Multinational corporations can transport capital and technology quickly to any place in the world, primarily to obtain lower labor cost. They seek countries where, at least temporarily, there are no minimum labor costs and work standards. Such transfer may benefit consumers and low labor cost economies for a short period, but the question can be raised as to whether this is desirable in the long run.

Clearly, new uncertainties are ahead in the world's trading relationships—and free trade of the old laissez faire private sector type is on the decline, and the invisible hand will be wearing hand cuffs. Big government has arrived on the international trade scene and maybe that's not all bad.

My second quote is from E.B. White to the effect that:

The future of complexity is bright.

White's statement of twenty years ago, describes so well the tangles in this second area of concern—the international commodities trading (oil, coffee, copper, nickel and other basic raw materials important to most countries of world). It involves the so-called North-South, Rich-Poor country confrontation: the rich countries of the North (at least rich before OPEC) confronting the poor countries of the South (at least those without hydrocarbons). The situation illustrates the difficulty of making economic progress in an interdependent world without an agreed internationally effective political mechanism. This discussion between rich buyers and poor sellers has been going on for a long time. Numerous recent expropriations have added an additional dimension of instability and intensity to the discussions. The suppliers of capital wish to be insured against this risk if they are to participate in a common trust fund operation.

But the South has decided that the example of OPEC is a triumph of Might and Right and should be followed in other commodity areas. These countries feel that the private sector has been rigged against them as producers of raw materials, and that as underdeveloped countries, they do not get their fair share of the profits on the commodities they produce. Their request is for a common trust fund to finance a price stabilizing mechanism to insure steadier and larger incomes for the poor countries of the South and steady supplies and higher prices for the North. The fund would buy when the market goes down and sell when the market goes up.

A report on the just completed UN session on trade and development (UNCTAD) to discuss this situation indicates that the requested new political mechanism for a new economic order for commodities is far from agreed. Even though the Carter administration seems inclined to make friendlier comments than the Ford people, as does the common market representative, the sides are, in reality, far apart.

A recent report, expressing the view of the South, said, "In Tanzania, we don't talk about benefits, we talk about principles." But a US official states, "our policy is reciprocal self interest."

So, an observer says about the conference, "This isn't even a dialogue of the deaf; it's people who are deaf talking to people who are blind."

Obviously, OPEC is operating an effective price-fixing cartel in oil, based on both economic incentives and political goals in the Mid-East.

A recent study by the US Government Commission

on Supplies and Shortages indicated no other commodities are likely to be subject to the same economics of scarcity as oil. To attempt to achieve an OPEC of copper, aluminum, bananas or tea, does not seem likely to be effective in the long run. Everyone favors help by the rich to the poor, but controlling the market through a common trust fund to help certain producers may be a very unfair and unequal way to achieve the results. Not only will some rich producers of the same product get richer (for example US copper will benefit us) but, in the end, the odds are that the common trust fund will lose its economic gamble with the speculators and traders of the world. Failure might be less assured if the fund could be operated on a non-political basis—but that is not a practical likelihood. The first time the fund's managers try to sell from inventory, lowering prices and thus cutting back production and employment, the full extent of the vulnerability of the fund to political pressure should be revealed. Stable commodity prices, through the use of a stabilizing fund, are a wonderful goal, if only we can figure out a way to prevent underlying economic reality and political activity from upsetting our apple cart.

Still, I predict some kind of very complicated governmental market controls and common trust fund will be forced in place by the South countries in the short run. The result will be more government controlled bargaining, and less of a free market. Complexity is on the rise for every business. Big government has arrived on the raw materials scene—and probably that's not all bad.

My third quote is from a distinguished economist, John Galbraith. It is:

We cannot have deficits in booms and recessions. Life is not yet that wonderful.

(Look at his new delightful book "Age of Uncertainty.")

This describes my concern with respect to the massive imbalance of international payment accounts. The debts between private and public organizations of one nation and those of another are at an all-time high.

Never have so many borrowed so much, with such poor prospect of repayment.

Serious imbalance is largely the result of the OPEC oil price increases. The effectiveness of OPEC concerted action is perhaps the most important international economic event of our lives.

The OPEC nations argue, rather effectively, that they are doing the world a favor by forcing conservation of a scarce world resource. They say they are controlling production, as the Texas Railroad did for years, to prevent wasteful production, where the cost of production should not be the primary determiner of price. Perhaps! But the result is the most serious world fiscal imbalance in modern times.

Thus, the most immediate problem facing the economies of the world today is finding a way to pay for the high cost of oil. World dependence on this finite resource for energy has been a well known long-term problem. But I refer to a short-term difficulty: the prospect for default on debt repayment by a large number of countries, with resultant crippling of the world financial system. We'll not have to worry about freezing to death in the dark but we'll all be going broke in the full light.

A quick review of the facts:

International debt is estimated to be $250-300 billion, and is growing at the rate of $40-50 billion a year. The largest part of this growth is a direct result of oil price increases.

The Soviet Bloc's (heavy borrower) indebtedness to the world's industrial democracies is $30-40 billion, and is growing at a rate of $10-12 billion a year.

US foreign oil payments for 1977 is estimated to be in excess of $40 billion.

The International Monetary Fund (IMF), the principal governmental source of credit for oil, has total resources of 45 billion and only about 7 billion currently available for loans to meet oil payment. The Witteveen Facility hopes to add 9–16 billion more to meet the problem at hand.

World economic interdependence has resulted in debts between many types of nations: East and West; OPEC and oil consumers; North and South. Such a financial relationship, involving large amounts between adversary nations is unknown in previous history. To a large extent, this growth of debt is unregulated, and even, to some extent, unreported. No forecast to my knowledge exists that foresees a way to carry this increasing debt load for any sustained period. It is estimated that some 70 percent of the international credit has been provided by private banks. Many of our major US banks are earning more than one-half their income from international sources.

Recycling has been suggested as an answer. To recycle, creditor nations such as Arabia and other OPEC countries lend or invest in debtor nations, usually through the banking system. But, as Arthur Burns, Chairman of the Federal Reserve has indicated many times, recycling is not the long term answer. It is another word for increasing indebtedness. It is a way to get funds from the creditors to the debtors, but not a way to ensure their ultimate credit worthiness and their ability for repayment. Since the private banking systems of the free world have been the major vehicle for the cycle, they can be the first victims of default. The answer must lie in reducing reliance on credit, and substituting adjustment in the standards of living by transfers of real wealth to producers of oil. The solution requires tighter fiscal and monetary policies for debtor nations. It means they have to reduce their standard of living and this is unpopular and a politically difficult action.

In some less developed nations, there is no apparent practical solution. For example, if a nation with a sole export, such as sugar, which is now at an all-time low price, has a principal import such as oil, priced at an all-time high, the trade gap cannot be closed by selling more sugar, because the price of sugar is just too low—there just isn't that much sugar. They will have to borrow. Capital assets must be sold, but when they are gone, then what?

The Economic Summit Conference III in May probably will not talk a great deal in public about this problem—it could lead to too many extremely gloomy and confidence-shaking predictions.

As one who helped prepare the US delegation for the two previous Economic Summit Conferences, and attended both of them, my experience suggests that the financial balance of payments problem is the most urgent reason for the meeting in May, just as the Italian and British financial situation was a principal unannounced reason for the Puerto Rico meeting. This problem could become the "Vietnam" of the Carter administration, as the result of which, they may have to use their major resources and time on this unplanned and unwanted foreign problem, rather than on the main objective of a new and better society being built at home. —You can't increase debt forever—as we said, the world is not yet that wonderful. Here is an area where a big international goverment has made slow progress - and that is bad.

In summary, in trade we shall be seeing more governmental bargaining and less free private sector trade. In commodities and basic raw materials we see more governmental bargaining and less free private sector determination of price. And in trade indebtedness we see mounting imbalance and an urgent need for international governmental action. International economic relations are being recast in a way that increases the need for a system of international cogence. But the prospect for achieving such a system is uncertain in all areas.

This raises the question whether the new economic interdependence really is good for the nations of the world. It brings dependency which becomes increasingly risky as international governance falls further behind the events of the day.

Many have noted that interdependence of city dwellers has not necessarily proved an unmixed blessing in improving their way of life. The same problems arise for nations dependent on other sovereign states for important supplies or services. In the cities, the teamsters, garbage men, retail clerks, natural gas suppliers, and endless others, can bring the city to a halt in a short period of time by withholding their services. This power to strangle exists, even though we have plenty of domestic big government to try to deal with the problem of dependence. Internationally, suppliers of commodities, oil, financing, etc., can also strike and bring economic devastation to many countries of the world. There is essentially little system of governance to deal with the problem.

We should reexamine the need for nations or groups of states to determine if a more independent and less vulnerable status than today's is desirable. Should this sound like heresy and old-fashioned isolationism, it is not. It is a suggestion for a realistic look at what has happened, and to reexamine the old economic trade-offs. As Harlan Cleveland has stated, "interdependence is a fact, but each country has a choice with respect to handling the facts in their particular situation." That choice depends, to a great extent, on the amount of government they want involved in determining the degree of interdependence.

Thus the Chinese have tried hard to make themselves less interdependent and more independent. Given their circumstances and ideological views, that is understandable. Across the straits, the Japanese have created a prosperous and totally dependent society. Given their resources, primarily a skilled and productive labor force, that is also understandable.

In the US, we too, have a choice. By default in execution of policy, we have moved toward more dependency on foreign oil and trade imbalance. But we are brought to our present position, not by choice, but by procrastination.

Remember what F.D.R. said to the Congress in a speech in 1939,

> Our energies are not inexhaustible, and yet we permit waste in their use and production. . . .

And he called for legislation "to carry forward a broad national program of conservation of energy resources."

In the future, leaders of government and the private sector take it upon themselves to become aware of this, to become accustomed to judging all international economic activities in terms of whether interdependence means dependence or improved economic performance. Shall our shoe industry be eliminated by foreign low-cost products? Do we need a sugar industry more than low-priced sugar? Can we pay the price demanded for cartel oil, or was "Project Independence" in energy the right approach? These are governmental decisions which must be faced in a choice of policy.

A review of the international economic scene gives one the clear impression that government, international governance, is also going to become big government with all its problems of bureaucracy, inertia and controls. For, like it or not, the times require government to do a lot of things that were unknown only a few years ago.

Domestically, we have seen the federal government in the last ten years either begin, or reform regulations of: the environment, employment opportunities, pension and welfare programs, energy, nuclear safety, consumer products, commodity trading, occupational health and safety, national highway traffic safety and mine safety.

Illustrating the growth in domestic big government, spending for economic regulatory agencies has increased from 166 million in 1969 for 8 agencies, to $428 million in 1975 for 10 agencies. For social regulation 1970 costs were $1.4 billion for 12 agencies, in 1975 costs were $4.3 billion for 17 agencies.

In 1970, big government issued 54,105 pages of regulations proposed by the federal register, and this increased to 72,200 in 1975.

In almost every domestic social area mentioned, the majority of Americans want their government to protect them and provide rules of conduct. The same majority will soon be calling for similar protection in the international areas.

Big government, domestically and internationally is here to stay. The environment will be protected and the international financeers will be controlled. Life is, and will become more complex but "The future of complexity is bright."

The principal danger is not that big government will eliminate the private sector and our freedoms through design, but rather, through ineptitude. Big government is a challenge. Bad government is the threat.

My experience has taught me that the government has not learned how to efficiently use the powers it must exercise. It does not know how to regulate effectively and efficiently. It is not well organized to provide balanced decisions weighing all the trade offs which are a part of our complicated society. The trade off decisions in international economics must be made by a process which considers all factors including domestic economics, national security, human rights, environment, energy, etc. Domestic decisions also require viewing a number of factors.

The great challenge to our society today is not to eliminate big government, though there are a number of places where it can be curbed such as its economic control of prices. But to make it work effectively, there must be good management within government, and a sound method of balancing the complexities of today's society. Good cost-benefit analysis is essential to sound decisions.

It is my view that government will learn how to operate effeciently and manage well, only if it is taught by our best managers from the private sector. The regulated must teach the regulators how to regulate. Principal among the regulators needing such help is the Congress of the US which often creates the problem of inefficient and unrealistic regulation by the legislation it passes.

From our industries and our schools of business and public administration, must come a new generation schooled to manage governmentally needed regulation and involvement in the private sector in a way that maintains our freedoms and the advantages of our free market capitalistic system.

Big Government won't go away—and it will always be a burden and a bother. The challenge to us must be to make it perform efficiently and sensibly in today's complicated world.

Soc
HC
103
B52